I LOVE
CROSS-COUNTRY

Coloring Book

Ellen Sallas

LRP

I Love Cross-Country Coloring Book
All Rights Reserved
Copyright © 2016 Ellen Sallas

ISBN-13: 978-0692644966
ISBN-10: 0692644962

Little Roni Publishers / Byhalia, MS
www.littleronipublishers.com
@LittleRoniPublishers

Written and illustrated by Ellen Sallas, a.k.a Ellen C. Maze

PRINTED IN THE UNITED STATES OF AMERICA

The cross-country jumping course always begins in the "start box." There, the rider's time is counted down aloud, and he/she must wait for "1" to exit the box. It is a good idea to exit calmly if possible. Many horses anticipate the forthcoming excitement and can explode out of the box at the release!

Upper level cross-country horses eventually learn to think for themselves when complicated questions are asked of them on course. This is especially true at water complexes when the questions come fast and the splash can cause confusion.

At most recognized events, spectators are corralled behind tape or rope to prevent them from getting dangerously close to the action. It is always a good idea to watch for galloping horses when watching an event at any location!

A ditch is the most challenging obstacle for a horse. It takes patience and skill to teach a mount to not fear the hole beneath their hooves.

Getting left-behind is common enough when jumping cross-country at any level. The key is to keep your hand soft so as to not punish the horse's mouth. Holding on with your legs and releasing with your hand will allow you to gather yourself upon landing and give the horse encouragement to continue.

The fall of a rider results in elimination. You will see many amazing "saves" at the water as athletic riders hang on and right themselves through the craziest landings!

If the horse runs through the rider's hand at the approach of any obstacle, you will see him/her half-halt their mount. This is done with skill, using the hand, leg, and seat to correct the horse's balance before reaching the next challenge.

When the course goes through the forest, you will have an abundance of shade. Be sure to consider that when walking the course beforehand. Varying shade and sunlight affect the horse's eye as well as your own.

The landing stresses the horse's front fetlocks, so conditioning year round from nose to tail is important for an injury-free event mount.

In eventing, the lowest score wins. This means the rider seeks to garner the fewest penalties possible. "Dismounting" at an obstacle constitutes a fall, which means elimination. Time to shake off the water, Number 33, and safely exit the course!

Jumping onto a bank is one of the more fun parts of the course. Jumping down can be tricky, as you need to keep your hand soft and stay over your horse's balance. Schooling banks at home will give you great confidence.

Bold jumpers are best for experienced riders. It is easy to be unseated by a huge effort if you're not accustomed to it.

A skilled rider uses his leg and seat to encourage the horse before an obstacle. At the water, the stick might be used as well. A gentle tap on the hindquarter is usually all an experienced horse needs to remind him his job at this fence.

In the United States, eventing begins at Beginner Novice Level, followed by Novice, Training, Premininary, Intermediate, and then Advanced.

The cross-country course is approximately 2-4 miles long and comprised of 24-36 fixed and solid obstacles. The difficulty and complexity of the course is dependent upon the level at which you are riding.

All obstacles are numbered and flagged. The right hand flag will always be red, and the left flag white. A good way to remember the correct jumping direction is "R" on "Right" and "R" for "Red."

Many obstacles test the horse's bravery, which really translate to the horse's confidence in his rider. The horse has to know you will always give him a fair question and only ask him what he can actually do. Jumping over a pile of logs into water takes a huge amount of trust.

A good course designer will use the terrain to differentiate between the levels. A Novice horse will jump a max log on a flat area, but an Advanced horse will be asked to jump a max log at the crest of a hill so that effectively, he is jumping out into space.

Designer creativity is never lacking on the recognized cross-country course. Jumping a car, tractor, or even a Jacuzzi with rubber duckies floating in it isn't too odd. These human elements do not distract the horse as they do us; the horse sees height and width and jumps. To an experienced event horse, duckies matter little.

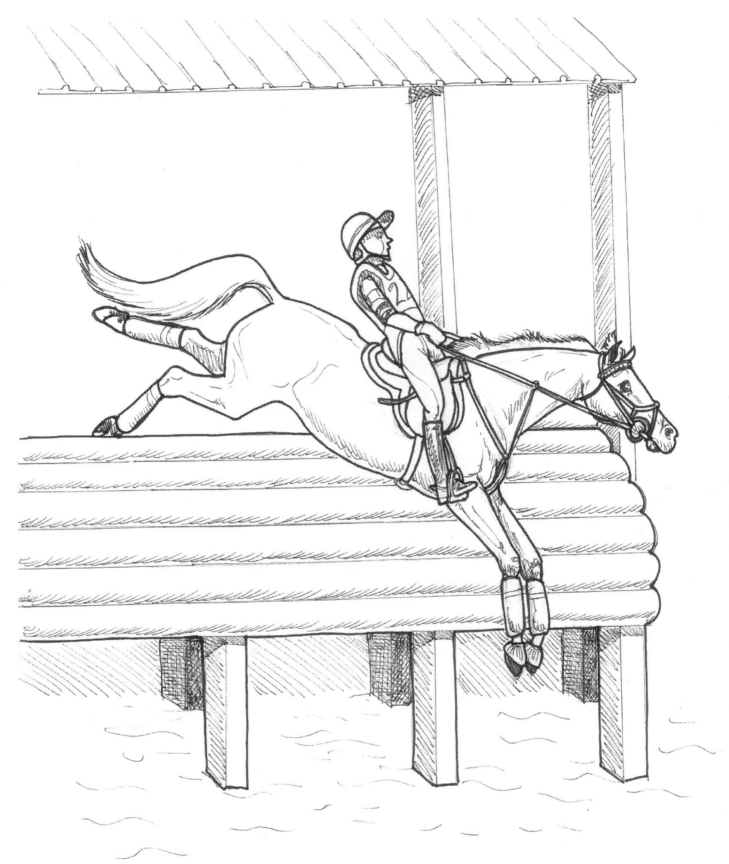

Competitors will walk the course 2-3 times before they jump it with their horse. This will enable them to decide on striding and make choices of which approach to use well in advance. Of course, you can't walk the water entrances, so practice at home and experience helps the most here!

Upper level horses rely on a strict conditioning program that includes flatwork. Dressage increases balance and response, and galloping work hardens legs and strengthens lungs.

At the upper levels, event riders require regular cardiovascular and strength training themselves. Many riders jog to stay in shape enough to gallop and jump four miles at events. It is quite a full-body workout!

Eventers love their mounts as partners, and you will often see them patting and praising them throughout the course. Horses respond to positive reinforcement at all stages of training.

Introducing the "thrills and spills" coloring book...

Look for these coloring books by Ellen C Maze (Ellen Sallas),
from Little Roni Publishers

- I LOVE RIDING LESSONS
- I LOVE DRESSAGE
- I LOVE SHOW JUMPING
- I LOVE TRAIL RIDING
- I LOVE PONIES
- I LOVE HUNTER/JUMPER
- I LOVE WESTERN RIDING
- BEEN THERE, DONE THAT
- COLOR ME SPLASHY
- EAT, SLEEP, HORSES

ABOUT THE ARTIST

Bestselling author and artist Ellen Sallas has been drawing horses even before she could walk. An avid horse lover herself, Ellen has been known to ride horses over hill and dale while daydreaming about stories yet written.

Ellen lives with her husband and vivid imagination in North Alabama.

Ellen and Amber competing at J3 in Mississippi

Ellen has sold her art worldwide as an acclaimed animal portraitist for nearly thirty years. You can purchase prints and originals at https://www.etsy.com/shop/giddyupstudio or by email, ellenmaze@aol.com.

CONTACT:

https://www.facebook.com/ellen.maze

https://twitter.com/ellenmaze

Ellen and Amber at Foxwood Farms
Eventing Barn in Pike Road, AL

ellencmaze.com

Read. Learn. Smile.   LittleRoniPublishers.com

COLORING BOOKS

New Imprint for 2018

FAITH

YOUNG ADULT

PARANORMAL FANTASY

LittleRoniPublishers.com

LRP

Made in the USA
Las Vegas, NV
13 May 2021

23005169R00020